*"I love*
   *because I have been loved.*
*I choose*
   *because I have been chosen."*

This book comes from the heart and
soul of a man who has seen life
and understood its lessons. Here are
the valleys and the peaks: insights into
daily life and problems, balm for
troubled spirits, answers for
all who question and examine their
faith. The poems in this volume speak
to us all . . . on salvation . . .
healing . . . repentance . . . faith . . .
choice and consequence . . . and those
dozens of daily experiences that
remind us that God is.
These pages contain nuggets—
PEBBLES OF TRUTH. Shelve your cares for
a moment. Browse and reflect with
William Stoddard.

# Pebbles of Truth

## William S. Stoddard

David C. Cook Publishing Co.
ELGIN, ILLINOIS—WESTON, ONTARIO

To my loving family,
and to a long-suffering secretary
who listened to the splash of "pebbles"
every Thursday morning.

# CONTENTS

# 1
# The Glory Way

## LET GOD USE YOU

There are two mind sets
    leading to two kinds of life
        and to two ends in life.
Like any fork in the road,
    these two courses begin close together
            and end far apart.

The one is determined to use God;
the other is willing to be used by God.
*Use God* when it is convenient or safe or useful
    and you will miss the glory,
                lose the blessing, and
                live in the shadows.

*Be used by God* when He wills and as He directs,

disturbing your safe routine,
upsetting your small comforts,
denying the less that He may give the more;
  then you will get the glory that
    transforms life,
  you will inherit the blessings
    that outlast life, and
  you will walk in the light as He is in
    the light.

Don't use God—that's a blind alley.
Let Him use you—that's the road to glory.


*


MAKE WAY FOR GOD!

So your heart is a desert—
  dry,
  lifeless,
  subject to flash floods of passion,
  but void of rivers that run deep,
                    stay long,
                    keep nourishing?

So your heart is a wilderness—
  rough with rocks of stubbornness,
  overgrown with brambles of fear and hostility,
  lonely with self-absorbing interests,
  haunted by bestial hungers that cannot rise
  above nature, red in tooth and claw?
                    then

*Make way for God!*

When He comes in Christ—
    the peaks and valleys of temperament
        will level off,
    the meaningless meanderings of self-seeking
        will straighten out,
    the rough relations with God and man
        will become smooth.

When He walks with you,
    your path is straight and level and smooth.
When He is denied access to your heart,
    your path is rocky, overgrown with brush.
    You stay in the desert and the wilderness.
    You *are* the desert and the wilderness.
Let the God who came to men, come to you!

### LIFE IS A LABYRINTH

Life is a labyrinth for everyone:
    We can stand still and feel the walls closing in,
    we can panic and waste our energies on
        frantic, fruitless searching—or
    we can move on with patience and purpose
        assured that there is one way out,
                one way through,
                one way, His Way!

Life is a labyrinth for everyone:
    Deafened by the empty echoes of secularism,
        the natural man listens not
            for the still, small voice of God.
    Relying on his own impulsive will,
        the natural man neither believes in
            nor cares about the painstaking instructions
            God has given in His Scriptures.
    Determined to do it his own way and
    worn out by as many errors as trials,
        the natural man refuses to heed that wise
            admonition,
            "When all else fails, read the instructions!"

Life is a labyrinth for everyone:
    Tuned to the Spirit of God through the
        Word of God,
        the spiritual man makes the right choices,
            runs with patience the race that is set
            before him,
            avoids the tempting bypaths that offer
            no exit,
            wastes neither God-given time nor
            God-given health
                in the pursuit of nongoals, and looking up,
            walks through the darkness toward the light,
                through the desert toward the oasis,
                through the trials toward the triumph.

Do you not suppose that the same One who says:
    "Come unto me, all ye that labour . . . and I will
give you rest" is also saying,
    "Come unto me, all ye that are caught in the

labyrinth and I will give you direction,
        I will go with you as you travel, and
        I will receive you at the end"?
And isn't that a good way to begin . . . "forever"?

### THE CALL TO LIFE

The call to Life is broadcast, as in radio;
The choice of Life is selective, as in radar.

The call to Life may be heard on all the bands;
The choice of Life is heard only on the frequency
   of faith.

That is why one is so general,
and the other so specific.
   That is why many are called,
   but few are chosen.

It is one thing to be among the many
   who hear the call of Jesus.
It is quite another thing to be among the few
   who are chosen to follow Him.

Granted that we have heard the call
   and our heart awakens with a desire
      to level with God and go with Jesus.

15

Granted that we want to leave
    the "low-vaulted past"
        and lay ourselves open to the risk of glory.
Granted that yesterday's victories
    have lost their sparkle and
        God's better tomorrow summons us
            to the venture of faith.
Granted all that,
    is it I who choose—or am I chosen?

Only God has the ultimate answer.
This one thing I know:
    "If I choose" to follow,
        early and thrilling will be my discovery:
            "I have been chosen!"

I love because I have been loved.
I choose because I have been chosen.

*

BLESSED IS HE . . .

"Blessed is he that cometh . . ."
    The love of God is such that to be blessed
    (or happy) He could not have remained
    aloof from His errant creatures, or
    detached from the pain that man's folly has
    caused and deserved.
        He had to come.

He had to move out of the awesome vastness
    of infinity,

He had to move out of the unsuffering bliss
      of Heaven,
He had to move out of the splendor of
      uncreated Light,
He had to come because He first loved us.
    There is no blessedness for love that will not
    take the risk.
        God knows that.
            We are the beneficiaries.
                But, in His coming, He too is blessed.

Blessed are they to whom the Lord cometh
    Imprisoned, they are released.
    Loveless, they learn to care.
    Despondent, they come alive with vibrant hope.
    Burdened, they feel a Hand that bears *both* them
      and their burden.

In blessing us, God is praised.
In praising God, we are blessed.

Try to make the sun go from West to East,
try to make the river run back to the spring,
try to make the blessed stop their singing or
      curb their enthusiasm,
and if you succeed—start listening—
for the stones at your feet are crying out!

## THE PRIZE BEYOND THE GIFT

"To the prize!"
What prize?

Salvation is not the prize "we strain to receive."
    A prize is what you get for striving or working;
    Salvation is what you get without striving
        or working.

Peace is not the prize "we strain to receive."
    A prize is what you get in competition
        and struggle.
    Peace is what God gives in spite of competition
        and struggle.

Acceptance is not the prize "we strain to receive."
    A prize is given to certain people and
        withheld from others.
    Acceptance is our assurance from God that all
        His children are special—not one is
        not special.

What then is the prize?

The prize is surprise!

The surprise of joy locked in the heart
    of sacrifice,
The surprise of freedom distilled from the heat
    of discipline,
The surprise of companionship on the road of
    lonely duty,
The surprise of being *with* God on the *way* to God.

The gift is ours for the taking.
The prize is ours for the striving.
Only certain people will get beyond the taking
    to the striving.
But then, only certain people will get the prize
    beyond the gift.

\*

REALLY IN THE FOLD

Jesus, our Lord, the great, good Shepherd
       has "other sheep."
       Does this fact bother you or thrill you?
       Does it leave you cold or make you warm?
       Does it lead to resenting or to repenting?

The way we respond to the fact that Jesus has
    "other sheep," and loves "other sheep,"
    is a clear indication of our own spiritual
    condition.

If we are not *really* of the fold,
    but only *think* we are,
       of course, we will not rejoice
          when others come in, and
          the place gets crowded, and
          our comforts get threatened.

If we are really in the fold
    and know ourselves to be truly His,
       we will rejoice
          when He reaches the lost, and
          when He heals the bruised, and
          when He companions the desolate.

If we are really in the fold
  and know ourselves to be truly His,
    we are willing to share Jesus with others,
    and eager to show Jesus to others.

Jesus loves "other sheep" than you,
  but, in loving them, He loves you not the less.

Jesus loves "other sheep" than you,
  but, if you cannot love them too,
    you must love Jesus less.

## WHAT GOD WANTS

What God wants to do for us
has to be wanted by us.
    It doesn't often come unsolicited
    nor does it ever linger unappreciated.

God, our Father, is not so different from us:
    He wants to be wanted.

Do we not find it better and
    should not God find it better
        to be invited than to invade,
        to be wanted than to be tolerated,
        to be welcomed than to be endured?

Do we not find it better and
    should not God find it better
        to be wanted for who we are
        than for what we can give?

God wants to be wanted.
    Sincerely wanting God means surely having Him,
    and having God, we will have no other wants.

"The Lord is my Shepherd, I shall not want."
    Having Him, I have all:
        all of Him, all of myself,
        all the best of this life and
        all the rest of Eternity.

Let God's wanting to give be matched
    by our wanting to receive.

It's a perfect combination
    with perfectly wonderful results.

## DEVOTION OR DISLOYALTY

Devoted to Christ—and satisfied.
Disloyal to Christ—and empty.
> This is the choice that confronts all souls,
> this is the crossroads that determines
> all destinies.

Devotion to Christ is life at high tide:
> free, full, and fresh.
Disloyalty to Christ is existence at low tide:
> stranded, still, and stagnant.

Devotion to Christ is a net that is full:
> gathering in life's richest treasures,
> garnering life's sweetest blessings.
Disloyalty to Christ is a net that is torn:
> limiting what little you can get, and
> losing what little you may get.

Devotion to Christ calls for a decision;
Disloyalty to Christ comes from no decision.

So,
Make a choice and start to live,
For,
making no choice is to choose to die.

## GOD'S GIFT OF HIMSELF

Mysterious beyond all understanding,
    yet real beyond all denying;
Higher than all human love,
    yet deeper than all human need;
Big enough for everyone to see
    yet small enough for anyone to receive:

"God himself—in Christ—bore our sins . . ."
    He took the shame
    and removed the blame.
      He endured the pain
      and erased the stain.
        He came all the way from Heaven
        to take us all the way to Heaven.

"God himself—in Christ—bore our sins in His
        own body . . ."
    not in the phantom pretense of a trick
      with mirrors,
    not in the shadowy substance of a
      strange dream,
    not in the mystical unreality of
      an apparition,
    but in His own body
      in the very body He condescended to use,
        with hands that gave blessing to
          children and sight to the blind,
        with eyes that saw beauty in
          everything and potentially
          in everyone,
        with lips that commanded a fever to leave

and a storm to cease.
in that body—in that very same body—
in that very real body—He bore our sins.

"God himself—in Christ—bore our sins in His own
body on the tree."
    First, He made the tree,
        then, He made the tree an altar of sacrifice
                            a symbol of victory, and
                            the key to the gate of Heaven.
No one can understand all that
but anyone can receive all that.
    God's gift of Himself calls not for
        understanding,
    just repentance, humility, and faith.

*

THE FREE GIFT

"The wages of sin is death; but
    the gift of God is eternal life."

Death is the earned result
    of standing in sin against God.
Life is the unmerited result
    of standing in grace with God.
As life and death cannot co-exist,
    so we cannot be at peace with God and
                        apart from God at the same time.

Where do you stand now? At this moment?
Holding in your hands
    the tawdry good works of fleshly pride,

24

the trifling excuses of human frailty,
the towering guilt of carnal weakness?
Then, receive what you earn
receive what you must . . .
"The wages of sin is death."
But
O thank God for that big little word!
O thank God for that Heaven-sent roadblock
on the boulevard to Hell!
O thank God for another way,
another chance,
another destiny!

"The free Gift of God is Eternal Life."
Eternal Life is the Gift of God—for it is
the source and substance of all other gifts.
What good is peace,
if it hangs by a thread in a nervous hand?
What good is grace,
if, like a stream lost in the desert,
it must finally go dry?
What good is hope,
if it is only a rainbow-coated bubble
that must explode in the wet silence
of frustrated tears?

Eternal Life is God's to give and ours to receive.
Why work so hard at failing
when we can gain so much by resting
in God, through Christ, forever?

*

## REPENTANCE

*Repentance*
>is the step we must take
to find the peace we would have.

*Repentance*
>is a low doorway
leading to high possibilities.

*Repentance*
>is man's need
and God's requirement.

*Repentance*
>is a word we understand very little
and like even less!

*Repentance*
>is not remorse—feeling sorry for the
consequences in our lives caused by sin.

*Repentance*
>   is feeling sorry for the sin
>   in our lives that caused the consequences.

*Repentance*
>   is not a passing emotion, a fleeting regret
>   or a trifling religious gesture.

*Repentance*
>   is thoughtful decision, meaningful purpose,
>   and presenting our bodies as a living sacrifice
>   to the living God.

*Repentance*
>   is a changed mind that finds expression
>   in a changed life.

*Repentance*
>   is a changed heart that bears fruit
>   in changed attitudes.

*Repentance*
>   has to be real to be really worthwhile.

*Repentance*
>   is saying, "God, You are right and I am wrong;
>   but Your right can vanquish my wrong."

*Repentance*
>   is saying, "I want that to happen."

*Repentance*
>   and life—and peace—and joy
>   is letting that happen!

*

CHOICE OR CONSEQUENCE?

The consequence . . .

        that means the thing that is bound to follow,
        as inevitably tied to choice and action
        as a shadow to an object standing in the sun.

Every man is free to choose:

    he may say "yes" when he ought to say "no";
    he may break the laws of nature and custom;
    he may parade before God and man in
        brazen defiance;
    he is free to choose.

But he is *not* free to choose the consequence of
    his choice.

    There his freedom stops.

        Choose the broad way—and it will lead
          to destruction.
        Choose the narrow way—and it will lead
          to life.

            Choose to live for self—and it will
              lead to captivity.
            Choose to live for others—and it
              will lead to freedom.

                Choose to live for Satan—and you
                  will dance to his tune
                  and at the end of his string.
                Choose to live for Christ—and
                  you will stand tall, walk free,
                  live in joy and abound in hope.

The choice is never beyond your control;
The consequence is always beyond your control.
The choice is yours and so is the consequence.
        The one you make—and the other you take!

## JOHN THE BAPTIST

John the Baptist wrestled with a choice.
He was engaged in a struggle.
    Every thoughtful person must
        at some time and often
        for some time
            be engaged in the same struggle.
And on its outcome rests
    our welfare now and
    our destiny to come.

It is an inevitable struggle and it is a real one.
    Here it is:
        "Am I looking unto Jesus?",
           an activity that is

sometimes difficult but
always fulfilling?
or "am I looking for another?",
an activity that is
sometimes the easy way out,
but always disappointing?

Which am I doing right now?
"Looking unto Jesus?" or
"Looking for another?"
John asked the serious question and
received the glorious answer:

Let the words of the Psalmist
find you where you are, and
lead you where God wants you to be.
"They looked unto Him, and were radiant!"

Believe this for a radiant joy now and
a radiant glory to come!

*

# 2
# The Love Way

## GOD'S LOVE

"Every one to whom much is given,
   of him will much be required!"

If God gave us much and required from us little,
   He would be neither wise nor loving.
      Loving, He gives to us;
      Wise, He requires from us.

A reservoir that takes in a lot and lets out but
   little ceases to be fresh.
      It changes from sparkling purity
         to dull stagnation.

The Dead Sea died because it kept all it received.
   It is a storehouse of fabulous wealth—but
      over its surface birds do not fly, and
      in its depths fish do not swim, and

from its saline fullness men do not drink.
Not willing to be used, it became useless;
not willing to give out, it had to give up.

God's will for us is better:
Not willing that we become stagnant ponds
or seas that die,
God lovingly supplies all our needs—then
wisely requires that we supply the needs
of others.

It's that simple.
God's love is wise.
Is our love real?

## I AM NOT WORTHY

"The thong of whose sandal I am not worthy to untie . . ."

Unworthy to do the most humble task.
Unworthy to perform the lowliest courtesy,
Unworthy to accept the most menial responsibility.

Far from being counted worthy to lead and
to command,

Far from having people regard my role as great
    or important,

Far from taking any credit or honor or praise,
    I am not even worthy
        to do the lowliest task
            of the lowliest servant.

But, thank God—
    My joy, my service, my destiny,
    My place in the Lord's kingdom now and
    My title to the riches of Heaven to come,
        do not depend upon *my* being worthy.


Jesus alone is worthy
    and in His worthiness I find my worth!

I am redeemed, I am considered important,
    and my role in life makes sense.

I am called out of the darkness of doubt
                into the light of certainty;

I am awakened from the death of purposeless
                    existence
                into a life of meaningful service;

I am summoned from the valley of discouragement
            to the heights of far vision
                    and calm assurance.

I am not worthy—in myself or of myself—not
                    worthy
    to be even the humblest servant in His Kingdom.

But in His love, I find my life.
In His will, I find my peace;
in His Kingdom, I find my place, and
in His worthiness, I find my worth.

## THE BLESSING OF LOVE

Self-forgetful, uncalculating, outgoing love is as prodigal as the fragrance of the rose. It just is. It is as unself-conscious as the smile of innocence quickly flashing across the face of a trusting infant. It turns not inward to reflect either on its own insecurities or on its own greatness. It does not make careful inventory of past grievances received or old favors given. It is like the sun that bestows its radiance and abandons its energies without asking if the recipient deserves them. What this world needs is love. How true! God showed the way in Jesus Christ. Have you found the Way? The way of love is the way to live. Find it. Follow it. Better, find and follow Him Whose sweetest name is Love. You will be a blessing to others. You will even be a blessing to yourself.

## THE GREATEST OF THESE

"And the greatest of these is love."

Love is the greatest thought:
    no philosopher ever engaged in more sublime
        reflection,
    no artist ever portrayed a more beautiful theme,
    no poet ever trembled on the brink
        of a more exciting discovery.
                Love is the greatest thought.


Love is the greatest fact:
    not the judgment we deserve to receive
             and are so quick to give,
    not the aggressiveness and greed
        that impel the success-oriented fool,
    not the security blanket of "things"
        that comfort the immature,
    but, undergirding and overarching all things,
             Love is the greatest fact.


Love is the greatest force:
    arguments are soon exhausted and always
        exhausting,
    hostility is a sword that cuts the user first
        and worst,
    pride sets its own trap and envy digs its
        own grave,
    but Love has neither fear of need
             nor need of fear.
             Love is the greatest force.

Love is the greatest act:
  "For God so loved the world that He gave His
  only begotten Son . . ."

Love is the greatest response:
  He who says he loves God should love his
    brother also.
  He who really loves God does love his
    brother also.

But, alas!—it's true—
Love is the greatest need:
  in too many lives, in too many places, in
    too many ways.

                    *


CHRISTMAS COMES BUT ONCE A YEAR

"Christmas comes but once a year"
  But Christ is always coming;
Just when we need His grace and good cheer,
  For our failure, His strong overcoming.
But so much depends on the state of your heart
  Whose door can be open or closed.
When He comes will He knock, then turn, and depart
  Unwelcomed, unneeded, opposed?

"Christmas comes but once a year"
  But that "once" would be all that you needed
If its coming brought with it all simple and clear
  God's love no longer unheeded.

## IF YOU LOVE ME

Love is born in Heaven and grows up on earth.
Love—in its essence—is God.
Love—in its expression—is God helping
   some of His children to care about all of
   His children.

Love is not made of gossamer dreams or
   beautiful words;
It is made of practical deeds
   for people with real names and great needs.

Love is not sitting in some pleasant spot
   in the garden,
   absorbing the healing rays of a kindly sun;
It is walking into unpleasant situations in a wild,
   wet wilderness in order to be healing sunlight
      for a lonely, suffering soul.

Love is not nice words promising great things;
It is good works performing little things.

Love is not a fleeting sense of well-being;
It is a daily walk of determined discipleship.

Love received and not shared is a cut flower
   whose beauty is real—but fleeting.
Love received and shared is a living plant
   drawing fresh strength and yielding
   fresh blossoms.

Jesus saw love not in terms of idle conversation;
He saw love in terms of living conduct.
      "If you love me, keep my words."

Jesus took love out of the ivory towers
    of pleasant speculation;
He put it on the hard road
    of simple obedience.
Yet that hard road leads to glory,
    that unpleasant task leads to comfort,
    that willing struggle leads to peace,

Love on earth is the road to Heaven.
Heaven came to earth
    planting love's seed in the world's need;
Now let us get on to Heaven
    sharing love's harvest with the world's needy.

*

## MORE AND MORE

"More and more"
"More" is one of life's crucial words
    It is good news and bad news!
More practicing brings the artist out of the crowd
More training keeps the runner ahead of the pack
More discipline molds a child who will not disgrace
        his home.
Yet, a glutton craves more and more food
        and finds it satisfies less and less;
    a hedonist lives for more and more pleasure
        and dies inch by inch in more boredom;
    a covetous person fills his hands with
        more things,
        and leaves his heart with more emptiness.
Everything in life is "more" today than it was
        yesterday.

We are more critical or more loving.
We are more resentful or more content.
We are more condemning or more forgiving.
Since life is always changing,
    and from day to day is more of one thing or
        another,
        it is of highest concern to us to determine
        what we are wanting more, getting more,
        being more.
So you're getting more interest on your investments?
                        That's not important.
What are you doing with more interest on
        your investments?
                        That *is* important.
So you want more years added to your life?
                        That's not important.
What are you doing with the more years
    that God may add to your life?
                        That *is* important.

If you want a kind of "more and more" in your life
    that is always satisfying but never satisfied,
If you want a kind of "more and more" in your life
    that will keep you alert to life's very best
    yet never surfeited with life's degenerating
        luxuries,
        I have a word for you from Paul:
           "That your love may abound more and more"
To abound more and more in love
    is safe and sensible and fully satisfying.

Try it!            You'll like it.

## LOYAL OBEDIENCE

As I pondered the word "loyalty," it seemed at first to be an overworked cliche that had long since lost its sting. It is one of those many slippery words: so easy to say, so hard to mean. I had to get a handle on it. In a flash, it came. The secret is in the word itself: L-O-Y-A-L—in *Loving Obedience You Are Loyal*. There is no other way. Love and obedience must flow together before we can get on with the rest of the word. In the very passage where He talked most about who were His friends, Jesus put love and obedience together, and never again should they be thought of as separate entities. A marriage took place between love and obedience and the result was loyalty. "If you love me, you will keep my commandments." Love based on anything less than obedience is mere sentimentality. Obedience based on anything less than love is mere bondage. Love without obedience is a fire without a furnace. Obedience without love is a furnace without a fire. Love without obedience is fuel without an engine. Obedience without love is an engine without fuel. Love is a blood transfusion still in a jar. Obedience is the arterial system of a human body. Loving obedience is a blood transfusion coursing through the veins and arteries. Loving obedience is life. Loving obedience is the most distinguishing characteristic of the loyal Christian. Think of this on Sunday; think of this on Monday; think of this on Tuesday; think of this every day:

In *Loving Obedience You Are Loyal*.

### GOD'S GRACE

Man's sin is
      solitary confinement
      in a stifling cell and
      in servitude to the sordid.

God's forgiveness is release from
      the cell of self
      to serve the suffering
      in surprising satisfaction.

Sin is darkness
    settling over the narrow tomb
      of a heart that has
        kept God out.

Grace is light,
    bursting the narrow tomb
      of a heart that God may
        let man out!

# 3
# The Light Way

### God Is Light

God is Light.
In Him is no darkness and
In Him we have no darkness.

So
Do not fear the darkness
for in God darkness cannot be.

And
Do not love the darkness
for in darkness God cannot be.

## SONS OF LIGHT?

Every Christian is a son by God—
> that is, God brings about the New Birth and
>> imparts His own life to him,
>> endowing like qualities,
>> developing like traits and
>> fostering like gifts.

Every Christian is a son to God—
> that is, God regards him as His own son,
> with all that that implies
>> in terms of responsibilities and privileges,
>> in terms of hard disciplines and ultimate glory,
>> in terms of little duties and great destiny.

Every Christian is a son for God—
> that is, God allows and expects him,
>> as a son, to
>>> act with love,
>>> to serve in His name, and
>>> to live to His glory.

It's our very nature.
It's something we can't help.

It's something we can't help, but we can hinder.
> Even God's light in us can be
>> hidden by selfish fears,
>> distorted by selfish ambitions, and
>> dimmed by selfish neglect.

All Christians are sons of light
but not all Christians are shining
> like sons of light.

Are you?

## THE DAY IS AT HAND

Those who turn their backs on Christ,
    refusing His way and choosing their own
        will get both what they want and what
        they deserve.

Those who want to hold on to the night
                and to hold back the day,
    are working against the grain of the universe;
        the light God created is never going to
            yield to darkness.

Those who love darkness will find it—
    and they won't like it.
Those who long for the day may be sure of
    its coming,
        and in it they will find and give a blessing.

For the Christian, the day is at hand.
    The only thing that is "far gone" is night.
        The Sun of Righteousness is risen with
        healing in His wings.
        The supply of strength is being
        ever replenished,
        the spring of joy is being continuously
        renewed,
        the cup of blessing is always being filled.

The night is far gone—let it go
                and let go of it.

The day is at hand—take hold of it
                and let it take hold of you.

The day is God's doing—
    He made the light that makes the day.

The day is God's way—
    walk in it.

Have a good day!

\*

## THE WAY IT IS

The light does not say, "I think I will start
to shine."
    No, if it is light, it gives light.

The city on a hill does not say, "I think I will
start to be seen."
    No, if it is on top of a hill, it shows.

The Christian who loves the Lord does not say,
"I think I will start letting my light shine
and my life show."
    No, if he loves the Lord, his face does shine
    and his conduct does show.

Come to think of it—whether he loves the Lord
    or not—something shines and something shows.

Only—if he loves the Lord, the light shines
    and shows Jesus!

That's the way it is.

### DAWN IS COMING!

In these ever-shortening days of autumn,
    one does not have to awaken too early
        to discover that he is still surrounded
            by darkness.

One morning as I looked out
    on a day that was still night,
        the expected and welcomed dawn
        seemed a long way off.

It was then that I heard
    the chirping of birds in our garden
        cheerful, sprightly, and a little fussy.

Their message to me from out of the dark silence:
    "Even though it is still night,
        dawn will come."

So it is with the promises of our Lord
    Like bird song in darkness,
        His promises assure us that dawn is coming,
           inevitably,
               gloriously,
                  and soon!

### THE BRIGHTNESS OF GOD

A candle is all right
    to help us move around in a dark room.

An electric lamp is all right
    to illuminate the pages of a book.

A revolving beacon is all right
    to guide an airplane toward an airport.

The moon is all right
    to cast a romantic spell on sweethearts
    who want
    to be alone—together.

The sun is all right
    to subdue night's darkness and
    to scatter morning mists.

**But**

Only Christ, in the brightness of His glory, in
the steadfastness of His mercy and in the power
of His love,
Only Christ is sufficient to bring saving light
to sinning souls and to scatter all the gloom of
all our guilt for all eternity.

It is the brightness of God's glory that is seen
in the face of Jesus Christ.

\*

TREAT LIGHT WITH RESPECT

You opened your eyes this morning and, sure enough,
there was light.

But are you sure enough of what you are doing with
the gift of light?

Light is a gift, you know. You didn't make it,
you can't destroy it.

But you can abuse it, waste, it, fool with it, and
hide from it.

Treat light with respect. Sometime, the gift
disdained will be the gift withdrawn, and then
you will long for the light you despised and
you will hate the darkness you have loved.

\*

## SHINE THROUGH ME

"You are the world's light."

"Who, me?"

"Yes, you."

"Isn't that a pretty big order, Lord, for an ordinary guy? The world is huge and I'm not even shining very well on my own street or in my own home. I couldn't pull it off."

"I'm not asking you to be big enough to do the job. Bigness doesn't count anyway—neither the bigness of the world nor the bigness of your light. It's faithfulness that counts. All the darkness in all the universe can't conquer the light of a single candle. I only ask you to share my love and square with my truth—then you can't help it, you *will* be the world's light."

"Here am I, Lord, shine through me."

*

# 4
# The Good Way

## THE GREAT RESTORER

"Restored"—what a beautiful, comforting word!
    It is all sunshine and gladness.
    Restoration is a word to lighten the heavy load
           and to brighten the heavy heart.
It is God's good word and God's good act—in Christ.

Body tired—mind weary?
    Night comes and rest—
        God restores strength.
Spirits down—faith burns low?
    The Scriptures are read—
        God restores hope.
Trials mount—sorrows flood?
    The Comforter, promised, comes—
        God restores peace.

God is the great Restorer:
    The dim outlines of a vanishing hope,
    the dull surface of a tarnished faith,
    the dying flame of our first love for Christ
        may need restoring and
        will get restoring
            when the roadblocks on God's highway
            into our hearts are all removed.

\*

FORGIVENESS

Forgiveness is the key to life:
    It opens our hearts to God
    and shows God's heart to us.

Forgiveness is the key to life:
    It locks the door on our past—
        miserable, apart from God
    and opens the door on our future—
        beautiful, united with God.

Forgiveness is the key to life:
    it provides the reason
        and the strength to try again.
    "This time we'll make it because—
    incredible mystery—
            we are important to God and
            He believes in us."

Forgiveness is the key to life:
    Christ gave His life to give us life;
    that is the cost and that is the glory
                of forgiveness.

Take the key—it's free
But do not take it lightly—it's not cheap!

\*

### SEVENTY TIMES SEVEN

To Jesus, forgiveness was not a mathematical
　　　　formula
　　　　　　written with chalk on a board,
　　it was a necessity of love
　　　　　written with blood on a Cross.

To Jesus, forgiveness was not an experimental
　　　　hypothesis,
　　it was an experienced reality.

He never had to ask for it, but He was always
　　　　　　　　　giving it.
Isn't it strange that we who need to ask for it
　　are often slow in giving it?

"I've taken just about all I intend to take.
The next time . . ."
　　　　　　"Seventy times seven," said Jesus,
　　　　　and set His face toward the Cross.

"You don't expect me to be a doormat, do you?
I'll give him one more chance, but then . . ."
　　　　　　"Seventy times seven," said Jesus,
　　　　　and set His face toward the Cross.

"Forgiving the unforgivable is hard."
　　　So was the Cross: hard words, hard wood,
　　　hard nails.

"Going the second mile is too much to ask."
>So was Gethsemane and the bitter cup,
>so was the thorny crown and the flesh-tearing
>>whip.

But as beyond the Cross, there was the
>>Resurrection,
>as beyond the shame, there was the glory,
>as beyond the humiliation, there was the
>>exaltation,
>as beyond the defeat, there was the victory,

So also beyond the taking of injury,
>>there is the gift of healing,
>and beyond the doormat,
>>there is the door to life,
>and beyond the pain of forgiveness,
>>there is the joy of reconciliation,
>and beyond the second mile,
>>there is rest.

"Seventy times seven"? Forgiveness is
>>not legal bookkeeping!
All the records of our carefully noted injuries
will be closed, when the heart is truly
>>open—to God.

*

## LISTEN TO HIM

"Listen"—
    God gives us hearing, then tells us to listen.
    Hearing is His gift, listening is our response.
        Hearing is general, listening is specific.
        Hearing is involuntary, listening is
            intentional.
    We hear anything that makes a sound;
    we listen only to what we want.
        We hear the freeway rumble and the
            rush of wind;
        we listen to the radio or the talking
            of a friend.
We hear the minister speaking or the choir singing;
we listen for God's special word to us
        a word to change a drab Now
            into a beautiful Forever.

"Listen to Him"—
    Since hearing is what God gives to us and
    since listening is what God commands from us
        since we have little control over hearing and
        since we have much control over listening
    everything depends on the object toward which
    our "hearing" device is pointed in the act
        of "listening."

We can listen to the arguments of doubt,
we can listen to poisonous gossip,
we can listen to our own cowardly fears
              or
we can listen to *Him*.

You *must* hear everything but
you *may* listen only to Him.
    then
        Beyond hearing will be listening,
        and through listening will be faith,
        and through faith will be
            the peace of a wonderful Now and
            the assurance of a beautiful Forever.

*

## WE ARE NOT DESOLATE

"I go to the Father"
    Gone, the familiar, friendly face;
        the compassionate, healing touch;
        the kind, encouraging voice.
    Taken from their sight,
      lifted above their reach,
        carried beyond their hearing.
    Looking up, the earthbound saw Him go:
      To have been forever, He was now no more.
    Clouds closed in,
      The image of their ascended Lord
      lingered for a moment against the
          contrasting dark.
        They watched intently the spot;
        then even that disappeared
          devastating nothingness,
          crushing loneliness,
          bewildering desertion.
    Ascension to the Father?

Is that desertion of the disciples?
No,
No,
*No!*
"I will not leave you desolate"
All that His physical Presence could mean
only more—would be ours in the Gift of the
Spirit,
more friendship, more healing,
more comfort.
The Spirit given and given for keeps
not for an instant, withdrawn;
not for a moment, departing,
not for a second, unavailable.
The abiding joy of Christ's friendship,
the continuing power of Christ's healing,
the sustaining grace of Christ's words.
Here even more than there,
now even more than then,
ours even more than theirs.
We are not desolate.
We are rich beyond all reckoning,
blessed beyond all dreams,
secure beyond all fears,
befriended beyond all desertion.
We are not desolate—He didn't leave us that way!

GOD SPEAKS TO US

God shows Himself to us in many ways,
    yet there are many who say, "I cannot see Him."
God speaks to us in many ways,
    yet there are many who say, "I cannot hear Him."
God shows Himself to us
    in the clean slate of a new day,
    in the self-forgetting duties of a busy day,
    in the good tired of a long day.
God speaks to us
    in the spontaneous laughter of childhood,
        unshadowed by cares;
    in the strong resolution of youth, wrestling with
        the worst and believing in the best;
    in the wise calm of age, knowing that no storm
        lasts forever, and
    beyond the clouds, there is always the sun.
God shows Himself to us
    in the small seed that loses its identity in the
        caressing earth,
    in the powerful life-thrust that lifts heavenward
        a delicate blade of common green,
    in the splendid gift of flowers full grown in the
        pure ecstasy of color.
God speaks to us
    in the counsel of trusted friends and in the trust
        of loving kin;
    in the Book of books that is needed so much and
        heeded so little,
    in the beautiful Life of the fairest Prince of
        Heaven and the truest Friend of man.

God remains invisible and silent—not to those
        who cannot—
            only to those who will not—see Him
        or hear Him.

\*

## DOUBLE STRENGTH

The strength God gives is "double strength"!

It is internal and external.
The strength of God comes to the surface of life
    from the depths within.
Like a seed sprouting from the silent dark,
    so the strength of God is born in my heart.
Like a root reaching out to give unseen support
    so the strength of God bears up my heart.

The strength of God is external.
He not only "fills me with strength,"
He also, "protects me wherever I go."

As a seawall breaks the fury of unbridled waves,
    so God makes of my heart a harbor for ships
        laden with calm thoughts of love and virtue.
As a shield turns back the swift, subtle arrow,
    so God keeps my heart safe from the accusings of
        conscience and the stain of unsurrendered
        passions.

"He will cover you with his pinions,
and under His wings you will find refuge;
His faithfulness is a shield and buckler.
You will not be afraid . . ."

His strength is double strength: strength within
and strength all around.

*

## TAKE CARE

"Take care of him."

Care about ourselves is something that takes us.
Care about others is something we must take.

Notice that the Good Samaritan is called "good"
by the One who knows what goodness is
because he takes care of his neighbor.

He takes the extra time—
It would have been easier to hurry on.
He takes the wounded body in his hands—
It would have been contaminating to some.
He takes his own supply of oil and wine—
It was probably getting low.
He takes his own beast to bear the aching,
weary stranger—
It meant he would have to walk.
He takes the money from his purse—
It could be argued that he had little
enough to spare.

Care is something we must take.
It doesn't just happen.

But, to the joyful surprise of many
who have taken the burden of care,
there is something else that is taken with it:

In taking care of others,
        we take, as a gift, the blessing of God.

When our hearts go out to others,
God comes in to bless.
       When we spend ourselves for others,
       we save ourselves for the best things
             life can give.
       When we lose ourselves for Jesus,
       we find ourselves for eternity.
Take care that you take care,
       then,
Take the dividends of joy
       that God is waiting to shower
            on all who see things His way and
               who see all other people
                   as equally precious children in His
                   family.

It boils down to this:
       Care is either something we take
           or something that takes us. Take your choice.

## PERFECT PEACE

It's not the absence of problems—
It's the presence of the solution, God.

It's not ceasing to work to strive, to conquer—
It's beginning to work, to strive, and to conquer
    with a purpose—God's Kingdom.

It's not seeking to be blessed and comforted—
It's trying to bless and to comfort—in God's Name.

It's not banishing from the mind all worry—
It's filling the mind with all hope—in the triumph
    of God.

It's staying the mind on God.
That's peace.

God said so
"He will keep in perfect peace (not partial,
not temporary, not vacillating, not blemished,
but *perfect* peace) all those who trust in Him,
whose thoughts turn often to the Lord."

\*

## FELLOWSHIP

"Fellowship" is a long word that covers a lot
of ground,
and in saying everything, says almost nothing.

"Fellowship" is an easy word
that is quickly used and soon forgotten.

"Fellowship" is a useful word,
once over lightly and it fills in all
the chinks.

"Fellowship" means everything or nothing,
depending on what we bring to it.

Paul associated the "fellowship" of our
Lord's sufferings
with the power of His resurrection.
Have we found that combination?

When the Apostles taught, they had fellowship
and when they had fellowship, they taught.
Have we found that combination?

When the grace of the Lord Jesus Christ
and the love of God are present, there is also
the continuing and constant "fellowship"
of the Holy Spirit.

Have we found that combination?

Let us take this empty word
    and fill it with great meaning!

We shall discover Resurrection power,
    if we are willing to be in the "fellowship"
    of His sufferings.

We shall possess Christian maturity,
    if we are willing to go on in the "fellowship"
    of the Apostles' teaching.

We shall receive and give the grace and
                    love of God,
    if our fellowship is really the "fellowship"
    of the Holy Spirit.

Fellowship?
    Go ahead, use it, but don't abuse it.

It is too fine a word to be spoken casually.
It is too precise a word to be handled loosely.
It is too great a word to be treated lightly.

*

# 5
# The Free Way

## FREEDOM IS NOT SPELLED "FREEWAY"

"Freeways"—where did we get the name?
    With their darting demons,
        who is "free" to relax?
    With their tail-gating tormentors
        who is "free" to drive at ease?
    With their swerving speedsters,
        who is "free" to enjoy the scenery?

Freeways—often necessary, but never safe:
    The price of getting from on-ramp to off-ramp
        in peace—and in one piece—is vigilance.
    The mood while getting from here to there
        is constant alertness.

Freeway—the very name is tension!
    How good to have them—how much better to

leave them!

Consider how wonderful to be "free of the
          freeways"—by choice
     Better the sound of great music in a God-given
          home
               than the whir of wheels and the din of
                    diesels.
     Better the sound of children playing in a yard
          than the monotonous moan of motors
               or the tiresome tone of tires.
     Better the sound of your voice praising God
          than the sound of your voice raised
               in angry impatience over
                    the tangle of traffic or
                    the dullness of Sunday drivers.

Freedom is not spelled Freeway:
     Make a good part of your weekend available
          to your family and find each other.
     Make a good part of your weekend available
          to God and find yourself.

Freedom is not spelled Freeway:
     "He who does not gather with me scatters . . ."
     "Scatter" with speed-crazed freeway fanatics
          and miss God's best for you and yours.
     "Gather" your family, gather with God's family,
          and gather your thoughts—then count your
          blessings!

*

## FREE INDEED

"To be free!"—universal and timeless passion.

Whether true or false, the desire for "freedom"
        has prompted the decisions of men and plotted
                the courses of nations in every century of time
                and in every era of history.

Under this slogan, Adam rebelled,
        seeking false freedom and finding true bondage.

Controlled by this thought, the Prodigal Son
        left the kindly disciplines of home and
        found the bitter captivity of unbridled license.

Under this banner, Israel once defied the Egyptians
                and still does.

Invisible magnet on the ocean's lonely rim, it drew
        the Puritans to certain hardships in an uncertain land,
                to a life of deprivation, disease, and death
                and freedom.

"To be free!"—the timeless cry of every man.
"To be free!"—the priceless—but often disdained
                Gift of God.
We miss the true freedom when we miss God's freedom,
        No man is free until God gives him freedom
                through the only Liberator worthy of the name,
                Jesus Christ.

To be free is to be free to be—
        What God wants—what God wills—and what God
                makes possible in Christ.

Jesus answered them saying, "Truly, truly, I say to
you, everyone who commits sins is a slave to sin . . .
but if the Son makes you free, you will be
free indeed."

*

WORSHIP

Worship—the wonderful way God provides
to let self out and to let God in.

Worship is the way self gets out:
it pries us loose of our tiny concerns,
so big to us, so small to God;
it gives us a reason for being restfully busy,
not preoccupied with ambitions
that glisten brightly and fade quickly;
it helps us to assess correctly
all the empty goals
that demand so much and deliver so little.

Worship is the way God gets in:
not lost in the reaches of incomprehensible
space,
not trapped in the intricate delicacies of a
flower,
not confined to the regal majesty of a mountain,
but alive and warm and powerful and real
and nearer to us than breathing.

Such is the way, the wonder, and the worth of
worship.

When you find it, God finds you.
When you use it, God sets you free.

\*

## HE CARES!

Cares are bad;
Care is good.

Having cares that burden us—that's not Christian;
Having care about what burdens others—that is
   Christian.

Having cares,
   when God tells us to cast our cares on Him,
      is wrong—it's a sin.

Having care for others,
   when God tells us to bear one another's burdens,
   is right—it's the right kind of righteousness.

Reason:
   Since God cares for us,
   we are free to care for others.

   Since God has cared for us through others,
   we must care for others through God,
      through God's help,
      by God's command, and
      to God's glory.

He cares!
   Do we?

Joseph heard and heeded the Angel's command: "Rise,
and flee."
The best way to thwart the evil intent and
to escape the jealous rage of a king
gone mad, was to flee!

To have stayed around, expecting some miracle,
defying evil, and
daring the Devil
would have been folly.

Fleeing made sense and
made possible a better plan by God.

There is a time to stay and a time to flee.
It is not always heroic to stay around and
It is not always cowardly to run away.

The same Scriptures that counsel us to stand
against the
wiles of the Devil, tell us also to flee from
idolatry,
fornication, the love of money, and youthful
lusts.

If we have a vulnerable side—a portion that is
not yet
covered with the armor of God—fleeing makes
sense.

Until we are able to stand—with God's covering
of conquering grace and prevailing purity—
fleeing makes sense.

And, never, never, never does God counsel us
    to walk into the snare of the Devil
    to prove His strength or ours.

When you can run away from evil—do it!

When you have to stand against the Devil—do it!

God is honored, obeyed, and pleased in both:
    standing or fleeing
        if we stand when we should stand and
        if we flee when we should flee, and
            never look for ways and means
                to mix them up!

*

## THE WINGS OF AN ANGEL

"If I had the wings of an angel,
over these prison walls I would fly . . ."
    So runs the lament of a prisoner in a ballad
    that tumbles down the long steps of memory.

We all know the feeling:
    Around us are walls, so high, so thick . . .
        an unbreakable habit,
        an unrelenting pain,
        an insoluble problem.

    Around us are walls, so cold, so grim . . .
        an overbearing parent,
        a rebellious child,
        an inattentive friend.

"If I had wings . . ."

I would find no obstacle too great to conquer,
I would find no pain too great to suffer,
I would find no loneliness too great to bear.

"If I had wings . . ."
I would be free to love
     and to be loved,
I would be free to lose my old self
     and to find my true self.
I would be free to leave the past
     and to welcome the future.

"If I had wings . . ." This is wishful thinking.

You do have wings . . . This is actual fact.

They who look to the Lord,
    they who obey the Lord,
        they who surrender themselves to His
                perfect plan,
        they who wait for the Lord,
           they shall mount up with wings.

This is no idle promise.

So stretch out the wings of your faith
to catch the updraft of God's love
          and over all prison walls you will fly!

*

BORN AGAIN—FREE!

Sin doesn't stop with sin.

It is growth—multiplication—chain reaction.
Like a set of dominoes, all set on end,
   topple it here,

and away it goes, not to end until the last domino
falls.
The only thing that can stop the falling dominoes is
a barricade: a hand, a ruler, something from above,
something other than dominoes, something that
stands in the path.

The power of the Life-giving Spirit—through Jesus
Christ—is the only adequate and unfailing
barricade to stop the chain reaction of sin.

What He did on the Cross can keep the rest of our
life's dominoes from falling.

He was bruised for our iniquities.
Pray for His intervening grace, trust in His self-
abandoning love, get out of the vicious circle that
ends in death.

Accept His deliverance. Possess eternal life.

We were not born free. But we can be born again—
free!

\*

LIVE AS FREE MEN

"Freedom" is a word that sets our hearts to ringing.
There is not an ounce of meaning
nor a feather's weight of joy
in any life that is without freedom.
Freedom as a word is a word
around which a whole nation can rally and
about which a whole nation can agree.

Freedom is the pearl of great price
    to those behind the barbed wires of tyranny
        and injustice and even
    to those behind bars of their own making.
Freedom is a familiar word, and a beautiful word.
Freedom is often on our lips,
    often on the printed page,
    often in the stirring song, but
        not so often is it understood
        and even less is it possessed.
Curiously, paradoxically, inevitably
    to be absolutely free is
    to be absolutely fettered.
Freedom that is absolute is absolutely terrible.
Freedom must feel the checkreins of discipline and
    order or its end will be destruction and chaos.
Freedom is a condition dearly bought and
    must remain an attitude under complete control.
So, to echo the words of Peter, "Live as free men!"
But remember it is more important
    to live as free men *should* than
    to live as free men *would!*
Freedom with discipline is
    to have a happy today and a bright tomorrow.
Freedom without discipline is
    to be unhappy and to spread unhappiness
    today, tomorrow, and always.
To live as we *should* is real freedom,
To live as we *would* is real bondage.
So "live as free men"—should—that's good.

*

# 6
# The Modern Way

## MISSION: POSSIBLE

"This tape will self-destruct in five seconds!"
    Holding our breath, we wait for the telltale puffs
    of smoke, and on with *Mission: Impossible.*

There is something else that will make
    Mission: Impossible.
It is the mind set on earthly things.

    Such a mind set cannot appreciate the possibilities,
                  appropriate the benefits or
                  apprehend the meaning
                    of the life God intends
                    and the life God blesses.
    Such a mind set, thinking to fulfill its own good
    is slowly drained of all good.

Such a mind set, thinking to find life its own way
                    is brought to death in every way.

"This type will self-destruct in five decades,"
    but it will self-destruct.

Don't be the type that self-destructs.
Don't be the type that makes Mission: Impossible.

Set your mind on God instead of gold,
                    on others instead of self.
Set your mind on what you can give instead of
                    on what you can get.

Then you will not self-destruct
and you will be a part of making Mission: Possible.

It calls for giving, but results in living.

                        *

WOMEN'S LIB

Women's Liberation?
Her liberation is being a woman.

The more a woman is a woman,
the more a wife is a wife,
the more a mother is a mother,
    The more liberation she has and
    the more liberation she gives.

She is not thus subjugated to a lesser status,
nor is she sentimentalized to a higher status,
    she is just what she was created
    and intended to be:

> a companion,
> a helpmate,
> the half that completes the whole.

She is fulfilled and fulfilling;
She is a joy to herself and to others.

Men and women as competitors?
> That is not liberation,
> that is miserable bondage.
Men and women as complements?
> That is liberation,
> that is joyful freedom.

*

## BLESSED IS OUR KING

"Blessed is our King!"        King?
Kings leave us cold—they had their day.
Since 1776, the typical American has had little time
> for the typical king.
Kings do not control us or threaten us or own us or
> tax us.
> They don't even concern us.
The Chief Priests said, "We have no king but Caesar."
We say, "We have no king, period!"
But wait—the Christian must put a postscript on
> that.
All that a good king used to be to his loyal subjects
all that—and much more—the Lord Jesus Christ is
> to those who love Him and obey Him and trust Him.
He is the King of Love

87

He provides the source of love and
        directs the course of love and
        rules by the force of love.
He is the King of Life
    He has conquered all the enemies of life,
        and lives to prove that Death, Life's
            last enemy,
        has forever lost his power to harm or
        to destroy.
He is the King of Peace
    A word from His lips and the seas are calm,
    A touch of His hand
        and the turmoil of the heart is stilled,
    A look from His clear, calm eyes
        and our fretful anxieties dissolve.
His throne is not an elevated seat in a dazzling
        room;
it is a simple place at the undisturbed center
    of a humble believer's heart.
His commands are not petulant whimsy,
    catering to the ego of a proud though
        frightened monarch,
they are the plain words of One who,
    having walked through Life's humiliation to
        Life's glory,
        knows the best way and the only way.
Ordinary kings don't make it with us anymore.
        Good!
But Jesus is no ordinary King and with joy we sing:
    "Blessed is our King!"
He is on the throne of the universe.
Why shouldn't He be on the throne of our hearts?

Odd, isn't it? We who can't remove Him from the
    first,
    May withhold Him from the second.

*

EVIL IN THE HEART

A good question: "Why do you think evil in your
            hearts?"
Do you not know that the heart is where it all
            happens?
    It is the throne room of everyone's life
        and on the throne, receiving honor,
        wielding authority, and making decisions,
            there is—inevitably—self or Christ.

Do you not know that the heart is where it all
            happens?
    It is the control center of everyone's life:
        what Houston is to NASA, the heart is to life.
        There one reads
                the warning signals of temptation,
                the "all systems 'go' " of conscience,
                and the decision to "abort" any
                mission that strays from truth.

Do you not know that the heart is where it all
            happens?
    Confuse the heart—and the purpose of life
            grows vague.
    Soil the heart—and the color of life turns gray.
    Divide the heart—and the strength of life
            will wane.

89

Do you not know that the heart is where it all
                happens?
    The mind only sorts out what the heart commands.
    The hand only does what the heart wants done.
    The eye only sees what the heart intends to watch.

A good question: "Why do you think evil in your
                hearts?"
    To think evil in your heart is
    to find evil in your life.
A reasonable alternative:
    Think good and live well,
    think love and live purely,
    think truth and live freely,
    think Christ and live—
        really live—
            now and forever!

*

BETTER BREAD

There is good bread for which we can pay good money.

But there is better Bread for which we do not, need
    not, cannot pay money.

There is bread that satisfies the body, for a time,
    and perishes with it.

But there is another Bread that both creates and
    satisfies the deepest hungers of the soul
    unconsumed and undiminished to Eternity.

There is a bread that is stored on shelves, waiting
    to be sold before it loses its freshness.
But there is another Bread that is more present
    than now, always within the reach of anyone,
    as fresh today as yesterday, and
    as sure tomorrow as today.

There is a bread that man must purchase again and
    again.
But there is another Bread, beyond all price,
    for which only God could pay,
    and which he liberally gives to all
        who will receive it in love and
            partake of it in faith.

Which bread do you want?
Which bread do you need?

    The answer, of course, is—both!
    The truth, of course, is—God provides both!

\*

## A GREAT IDEA

"That's a great idea! Let's try it."

Every family, every company, every church has used
    that expression and a lot of good has come out of
    it.
No worthy goal was ever reached nor any dream
    fulfilled that had not its origin in someone's great
    idea.

Life shrivels and closes in,
    buoyant enthusiasm becomes deflated apathy,

the walls of an imaginary contentment become
the walls of a real imprisonment
when we willfully shield ourselves from
the blessed nuisance of new ideas.

But, thank God, our faith does not rest on somebody's
great ideas—ours or anyone else's.
Our real life is not dependent on the currently
popular and swiftly passing ideas of men.
The latest idea, the newest fad, the most current
fashion can be as frothy and unstable as circus candy:
beautiful in anticipation,
nothing in nourishment, and, in the end,
a sticky mess.

I've got a great idea: let's stand firmly on God,
who is not "here today and gone tomorrow"
who promises much and delivers more,
who says He can and already has,
whose great ideas are great realities, and
whose best idea is the salvation of sinners
through Christ our Savior.
Good idea? Great!

*

PLEASURES AND TREASURES

What are you really "banking on" in this life?

Pleasure?
It's a misty cloud you can't hold in your hand,
it's a haunting dream you can't hold in your
heart,

92

it's a hollow pillar that can't hold you in a
 storm.

Success?
 It's a bubble that bursts when the company
  changes hands,
 it's an "Oscar" that winds up in a pawn shop,
 it's the smell of roses but the prick of thorns.

Money?
 It's the flame under greed that burns away
  virtue,
 it's the frost that blights the fresh bloom of
  a generous heart,
 it's a man walking into prison, locking the
  door, and
   throwing away the key—and doing it all
   himself.

What are you really "banking on" in this life?
Why live for something that's going to die?

To lay up treasures on earth is
 to have nothing to gain and certainly nothing
  to keep and everything to lose.
To lay up treasures in Heaven is
 to have everything to gain and certainly
  everything to keep,
  and nothing to lose.

When the pleasure of God is man's greatest
  treasure,
Then the treasures of God become man's greatest
  pleasure.

## GOOD AND EVIL

Good and evil are not just opposites,
　　they are opponents.
Good and evil are not just in contrast,
　　they are in contest.

They are not friends
　　talking over the back fence.
They are enemies
　　taking over the other's territory.

They are not things that we can take or leave,
　　they are things that take us and lead.

Good and evil are not idle concepts
　　that one can record in a book;
They are not entries on opposite sides of a ledger,
　　like so many cold figures:
　　　　"credit / debit,
　　　　　　good / evil,
　　　　　　　　　Get the sub-total.
　　　　　　　　　How do we stand
　　　　　　　　　　at the end of the month?"

Good and evil are not passive figures at all,
　　they are active forces.

If we go with one,
　　we are against the other.

Choose your partner.
　　You cannot have them both.
　　　　They don't get along together.

And when we try to make them get along together

Or when we think we can let them get along together,
we don't get along very well.

*

REAL NOURISHMENT

"Man shall not live by bread alone."

The Average Person:
    "This man shall not live by bread alone.
    You're so right.

    People in 19th Century jails might exist
    on bread alone—but live, never!

    Real living is
        in cake not bread,
            in turkey plus stuffing,
                in delectable delicacies;
        in wide-screen color TV,
            in stadium-packed super-bowls,
                in firmly packed weekend ski trails;
        in cars with extra flare,
            in boats with extra power,
                in cabins with extra class.

    Bread alone? You're right!
    I can't live that way."

The Aware and Hungry Christian:
    "Nothing physical or material can give me
        the life for which I yearn,
        the life I must have or die.
        Neither bread nor cake

95

neither pleasures nor hobbies,
  neither sporty cars nor fancy planes.
Knowing that it ends in frustration,
    disappointment, soul-hunger and death,
*this* man will not even try to live by bread
alone, but by every word that proceeds out of
the mouth of God."

That's real nourishment for real life,
 real help for real needs, and the
 real formula for real success.

# 7
# The Glad Way

## REJOICE AGAIN

You can say that again.
All right, again I will say rejoice.

Again and again and again I will say, rejoice
    until the one moment of joyful discovery
      becomes the confirmed habit of triumphant living.

Again I will say, rejoice
    because I have reason to rejoice.
Again I will say, rejoice
    because I have seen it:

Rejoicing is the key to the Christian's abundant
        life.

It unlocks the door to let him out
   from the stifling cell of self.
It unlocks the door to let him in
   on the sublime satisfactions of service.

Rejoicing is the keynote of the Christian's
      victorious life.
   It says: "I believe all is well because
         I know all will be well."
   It never gives up "under any circumstances"
         knowing God is "over all circumstances."

The Christian has no reason to be cast down
   because God has come down.
   In Jesus Christ, God dealt with our darkest
      dilemma—sin.
   In Him, God delivered us from our deepest
      despair—guilt.

So again I will say, rejoice.
   It's the only way to cry!

So again I will say, rejoice
   and bring His joy
      in my joy—to the world.

*

Rejoicing! It is the Christian's privilege.
    A sinner, redeemed,
        sees how much he is worth to God.
    A prisoner, liberated,
        knows the exquisite joy of freedom.
    A blind person, given sight,
        appreciates the gift of all beauty.
            Christians, rejoice because you may.

Rejoicing! It is the Christian's responsibility.
    We have been lifted
        beyond the reach of all enemies.
    We have been returned
        to pastures green and
        to waters that are still.
    We have a Savior who cares and a God who
      provides.
            Christians, rejoice because you should.

Rejoicing! It is the Christian's identification.
    It is the spontaneous fragrance of a flower.
    It is the natural radiance of a light.
    It is the inevitable overflowing of a cup that
        is filled.
            Christians, rejoice because you can't
                help it.

Rejoicing! It is what God does when He finds us.
    Do we need a better Pattern?
    Are we looking for a better reason?
    Can God be honored with anything less?

Rejoice, and again I say, rejoice!

## ONLY WHEN INVITED

When Jesus comes, sadness goes.

> He is born and the angels sing:
>     "Good tidings of great joy!"
> He comes late to a funeral
>     and conducts a resurrection.
> He goes through the gates of death
>     and shatters them with the glory of an Easter
>     morning.

Little wonder, then, that His first miracle should
        change
    an embarrassing lack into a satisfying abundance,
    a depleted stock into an ample supply,
    and mere water into the wine of gladness.

Little wonder, that His first miracle should
    occur in surroundings of anticipated happiness
    and result in unanticipated joy.

That is always His way:
    He takes happiness and makes it joy.
    He takes the good and makes it better,
    He takes the ordinary and makes it sublime,
    He takes water and makes it wine.

Have you a dull existence
    that He can turn into purposeful living?
Have you a monotonous task
    that He can turn into exciting adventure?
Have you a plaguing weakness
    that He can turn into triumphant strength?
Have you some water
    that needs turning into wine?

He is a good Guest, the best of Guests,
    but He comes only when He is invited.
He has invited you—the Cross His invitation—
    hand printed with nails,
    edged in blood more precious than gold,
    and sealed with promises more lasting than
    the heavens.

Yes, you are on His list of invited guests.

But is He on yours?

*

## GOOD NEWS

He who receives and believes the Good News
    is bound to discover the new good!

What he looked upon as bad becomes good;
    what he disdained as cheap becomes valuable;
    what he ignored as foolish becomes wise;
    what he despised as useless becomes important;
    what he feared as drab becomes beautiful;
    what he avoided as dull becomes exciting;
    what he sought as satisfying becomes old straw, and
    what he thought he had to have—or die—
        becomes as unnecessary as last year's dog license!

A Christian walks in newness of life:
    with all the beauty of fresh, blooming roses,
    with all the refreshing cleanness of high mountain
        streams,
    with all the excitement of Spring rising out of
        Winter.

Christ gives that kind of life to believers,
Christ lives that kind of life in believers.

# 8
# The Living Way

NEW LIFE

New Life?
    Well, to put it that way presupposes some
      important things:

New Life reminds us that there is a kind of life
    that is *old,*
      a kind of life which God wants to lay aside
        in order that He may give us the new.
          The worn-out is replaced, and
          the dried-up is replenished.
            The New Life is death to old debts.
            They are all remitted.

New Life reminds us that there is a kind of life
    that is monotonously the same,
      a kind of life which God wants to lay aside

in order that He may give us one that is
excitingly different.
Habit-bound weakness becomes heart-free strength,
self-centered worry becomes love-impelled service,
the joyless round of petty chores becomes
the purposeful investment of minutes and hours
and days all leading to an end that makes sense.

New Life reminds us that there is a kind of life
that is ruled by suffocating self,
a kind of life which God wants to lay aside
in order that He may give us one that is
dominated by liberating love.

The New Life makes saints who make sense.
Is your *now* life His *new* life?
He is willing and able.
But it takes two.
It takes you!

## LIFE WITH CHRIST

Life without Christ is like "evening shadows"
It is facing the sunset,
struggling to hold on to a few more fleeting
moments, since that's all one has before the
darkness sets in for good, and that's bad.

Life without Christ is like "withering grass"
It is just dying,
turning brown for lack of nourishment—
the best has been and nought remains but
tinder-dry extinction.

Life with Christ is like "morning light"
It is facing the dawn,
content to know that more light is coming,
a day all beautiful with work and love,
and in the end, no night, no night at all!

Life with Christ is like "flourishing flowers"
It is life unfolding
in subtle fragrance, vitally creative,
a joy to be, a joy to behold, a joy to be around,
and all that lies ahead is more!

"For me to live is Christ and to die is gain."

## GO UP HIGHER

"Friend, go up higher."

That's the way it always is with God.
    He raised up Christ from the grave,
    He lifts up the broken in spirit,
    He builds up His church on an immovable rock.

His ways are higher than our ways
as the heavens are higher than the earth.

But everything in existence wars against the
    "upness" that God intends and that God supplies:
        Left alone
            water runs down hill and
            mountains tend to flatten;
        Left alone
            high temperatures become cool and

low temperatures become warm.
All existence, remaining unchallenged and
unchanged tends to head toward the dead
mean level.

Only life—the idea, the gift, and the
essence of God—can counter the downward pull
of death-bound existence.

Only as we are willing
to become allied with that Life
which comes from God and leads to God;

Only as we are willing
to let our existence become impregnated
with His life;

Only as we are willing
to give up our ways that lead us down and
give in to His ways that lead us up;

Only then—but surely then—
we shall find ourselves bound for Heaven and
no longer bound by earth.

"Friend, go up higher."
God wants to be with you in the depths, but
He would rather have you with Him in the heights.

## GOD COMES TO US

God comes to us in so many wonderful ways . . .

Our eyes opening on the grace of just another ordinary
day is the coming of God.
Falling into slumber with the restful assurance that we
cannot fall lower than the everlasting arms is the
coming of God.

The sun making glistening crystals on rain-washed leaves
is the coming of God.
The rain falling with gentle, cleansing grace from an
angry cloud is the coming of God.

The guileless, sudden smile of a child's innocent
delight is the coming of God.
The eyes of old age twinkling with the good
surprise that the best is now and still is yet to be is
the coming of God.

And it's all spelled l-i-f-e.

That's what Jesus came to give:
the freedom to see life at its best,
and the freedom to be alive at our best.

## TWENTY-TWENTY VISION

Every Christian, from the unbespectacled to the
    tri-focaled, may have "20:20 vision."

How's that?

Well, first, there is (II Chronicles) 20:20 vision:

    "Believe in the Lord your God, and you will be
        established."

    In these confusing times when most people are
        looking everywhere for something to which they
        can cling and upon which they can build,

  in these bewildering times
      when things are seldom what they seem and
      high-sounding promises never seem to make it,

  in these unsettled times
      when nothing seems to stay nailed down and
      honor lies in shambles,
        you may have this (II Chronicles) 20:20 vision!

And then there is (Exodus) 20:20 vision:

"Do not fear; for God has come to prove you, and that
the fear of him may be before your eyes,
that you may not sin."

Every time God "proves" us, it is for a good reason.
Every trial, except those we create by disobedience,
is meant to bring us a clearer understanding and
a closer walk with God.
Every burden, except those we create by willful
rebellion
is to be seen as a blessing in disguise.
(Exodus) 20:20 vision keeps the fear
of God always
before our eyes to shield us from sin.
Show me 20:20 vision that is better
than that!

Finally, and best of all, there is (John) 20:20 vision:

"When he had said this, he showed them his hands
and his side.
Then the disciples were glad when they saw the Lord."

Every Christian has heard what Jesus has said,
on the pages of Scripture,
through the beauties of nature,
in the silent hallways of conscience.
Every Christian has seen those eloquent symbols in
his hands and side.
Every Christian, with the disciples of long ago,
may be glad, for when it comes to seeing Jesus,
only doubt and disobedience can alter this
(John) 20:20 vision.

Yes, your vision may be better than you think, and
your vision can be better than it is.

# 9
# The Only Way

## THE HOUR IS COMING

"The hour is coming."
Yes, there is an hour that is coming:
    A feast of joy
        across which no shadow can fall;
    A bond of love
        unshattered by weakness or sin;
    A land of beauty
        upon whose shore there will rest no stain;
    A kingdom of peace
        whose placid surface will always smile
            beneath a kind and constant Sun.
The hour is coming:
    Thank God for it, believe in it,
    wait for it, live for it, die for it.

But in one sense the hour that is coming
　　　　is the hour that is now!
　　That is, we don't need to expect, and
　　　　we shouldn't expect,
　　　　　　that all our happiness, all our rewards, and
　　　　　　all our joy will take place
　　　　　　　　in some distant hour, long deferred.

God wants us to taste His goodness,
　　　　to appropriate His grace,
　　　　to behold His glory
　　　　　　in an hour that now is!

Just as Jesus Christ is coming and now is,
so the "hour that is coming," now is.
　　Don't wait for Jesus to come sometime.
　　Jesus is waiting for you to come now.
　　　　The hour is coming, and
　　　　the hour is now.


*


THE GOOD NEWS IS

The Good News *is*.
　　The Good News is not *was*—it *is!*
　　　　The Good News is present reality:
　　　　　　It is not a faded flower that droops
　　　　　　in the vase of memory nor a haunting dream
　　　　　　　　that drifts through the vacuum
　　　　　　　　of hope deferred.
The Good News *is* because Jesus is.
　　He was and will be but best of all He *is*.

Do you know He is?
Don't reverence Him alone as the
all-sufficient Lord of yesterday.
Don't put Him away like an insurance policy
that will someday be valuable.
Discover that He is and who He is and why He is.
You may be sure that He is yours—
it takes only an invitation;
just make sure that you are His—
it takes only a dedication.
You are not in the know with Jesus
until Jesus is in the now with you.
The Good News *is*—praise God it *is!*
Now, do you know Jesus?
Do you know Jesus now?

YES OR NO

It's the little words that give clear directions:
Up, down, right, left, push, pull.
It's the little words that give urgent warnings:
Stop, look, wrong way, help.
It's the little words that say the great things:
Love, joy, peace, faith, hope.

Jesus used little words to give His clear directions:
    "Put out into the deep and let down your nets
        for a catch."
Jesus used little words to give His urgent warnings:
    "Judge not, that you be not judged."
Jesus used little words to tell of His great gifts to us,
       His great plans for us, and His great works
       through us:
    "My peace I give to you."
    ". . . that where I am you may be also."
      "He who believes in Me will also
        do the works that I do."

It's the little words that are hard to misunderstand.
    We can find a reason for faithless inaction
    behind a smoke screen of long and confusing words.
    We can answer polysyllabic commands
    with polysyllabic excuses.

But the only way to answer the little words of Jesus
       is with a *yes* or a *no!*

Jesus said: "Put out into the deep . . ."
    "Yes, Lord, I am safe in the deep and
        in the shallows I will miss the glory."
(or)
    "No, Lord, I fear the deep and I like the shallows."

Jesus said: "Let down your nets for a catch . . ."
    "Yes, Lord, I will let my nets down into the
        unseen depth. I will answer You in faith,
        my faith will be nourished by obedience, and
        obedience will be rewarded with results."

(or)
> "No, Lord, these nets are too nice, too new, too costly.
> > I can't risk letting them down.
> > And besides, I'm tired of fruitless trying."

When Jesus speaks to us simply,
> He expects a simple answer
> > as simple as *yes* or *no*.

### THE BEGINNING AND THE END

Let the mind roam to the end of its tether—the
immensities of space, real and actual space, still
lie beyond its comprehension.

Let the questing spirit listen for the last
> tick of Time's pendulum—
Human intelligence must humbly
confess its inadequacy to take it in.
Space and Time must begin and they must end.
But how?

It has to be, but it can't be. Where is the answer?

The answer lies in Him who couldn't be, but *is*.

Jesus Christ *is* the Beginning.
Jesus Christ *is* the End.

Jesus Christ is the only unquestionable Answer to man's unanswerable questions.

Beyond the place where all probing minds must draw the curtain—past or future—Jesus stands,
Alpha and Omega, before the past and after the future.

# MORE
## rewarding reading...
## from Cook

**FAITH AT THE TOP** by Wes Pippert. The author, a seasoned UPI reporter in Washington, D.C., takes us into the lives of 10 prominent men and women who dared to bring Christ along with them on their way to the top—like Sen. Mark Hatfield, Washington Redskins star Charley Harraway, former NBC-TV reporter Nina Herrmann.     75796—$1.50

**HOW TO ENJOY THE GOD STUFF** by Hugh Claycombe. Through sprightly, captioned drawings, the cartoonist-author shows us fresh concepts of the Christian life: new ways to see people as Jesus sees them, methods that can heighten our ability to love. Unique approach addresses our real feelings about ourselves.     75838—$1.25

**CAMP DEVOTIONS** by Dick and Yvonne Messner. Like Jesus, Christians can use the glories of nature as inspiring object lessons—on a mountain, during a sunrise, near a lake. Each short, one-subject devotional offers site suggestion, Scripture text, theme, and prayer. (Yvonne Messner is a camp founder and teacher of camping.)     75945—$1.95

**CAMPFIRE COOKING** by Yvonne Messner. Pack-along guidebook to fixing tasty, nutritious meals from scratch in the out-of-doors. What utensils are needed? What preparation and cooking methods should be used? Which recipes are best? How can a group get the most from its time and money? A lifelong camper tells you.     75937—$1.95

**YOUR TROUBLED CHILDREN** by Elizabeth Skoglund. In a book for ALL families, this counselor, who is also a Christian, draws from a wider-than-usual background of experience in problems of children, parents, and society. Citing case histories, she offers ideas for constructive change and the return to a useful place in society.     81265—$1.50

**THE 13TH AMERICAN** by Pastor Paul. Encouragement for alcoholics, and all who are concerned about them—a pastor tells how God helped him beat the bottle. Although well educated and respected, the author found release not through his own efforts alone, but through the help of God . . . and those who offered their strength.   72629—$1.50

**THE EVIDENCE THAT CONVICTED AIDA SKRIPNIKOVA** by Michael Bourdeaux. This book places its reader at the side of a young Russian girl on trial. She chooses imprisonment to the abandonment of faith in a story that challenges ALL Christians. (Bourdeaux is a worker at London's Center for Study of Religion and Communism.)   72652—$1.25

**LET'S SUCCEED WITH OUR TEENAGERS** by Jay Kesler. An eminent authority, the president of Youth for Christ International, offers a new understanding of the age-old but desperately new problems even the happiest of families must face: coming of age, discipline and love, peer pressure, drugs, alcohol, tobacco, the Church.   72660—$1.25

**THE PROPHET OF WHEAT STREET** by James W. English. In hard cover, it was the choice of six book clubs! English, former editor of Boys' Life, tells the story of William Borders, a southern black Northwestern graduate who returned to lead Atlanta's black church to revitalized faith, improved housing, new self-respect.   72678—$1.25

**WHAT A WAY TO GO!** by Bob Laurent. For adults . . . to pass along to young people! They'll like singer-evangelist Laurent's conversational style and understanding approach. Bringing new faith to thousands, he packs solid Christian advice under catchy labels like Saved, Satisfied, and Petrified . . . and Jesus Signed My Pardon.   72728—$1.25

**THE VIEW FROM A HEARSE** by Joseph Bayly. (Revised and expanded.) Facing the ultimate crisis of death: one's own, the death of someone dear. In this book, Joseph Bayly offers practical help in coming to terms with this too-real of matters, including thoughts on the stages of dying, suicide, explaining death to children.   73270—$1.25